AS Religion & Et

REVISION GUIDE

AS Level Religious Studies
Component 02

OCR B (H173, H573)

Matthew Livermore

AS Religion & Ethics for OCR REVISION GUIDE

AS Religious Studies OCR specifications and past exam questions © OCR Examination Board, used with permission. References are included from the Oxford English Dictionary, some meanings are omitted, changed slightly or added to. Bible quotes refer to the New International Version.

ISBN: 978-1-78484-143-0 (pbk)
ISBN: 978-1-78484-146-1 (hbk)
ISBN: 978-1-78484-149-2 (ebk)
ISBN: 978-1-78484-152-2 (kin)

Published in the United Kingdom by PushMe Press.

www.pushmepress.com

YEAH, WELL, THAT'S JUST LIKE

YOUR OPINION
MAN

Introduction to Religious Ethics

Students entering upon courses of study at A Level and undergraduate level very frequently hold some sort of relativist worldview. One of the strengths of this course is that it will seriously test such a worldview. The relativist view itself is not the problem, rather the unthinking assumption that relativism is the only rational option. As a teacher, I frequently experience "lazy relativism" by students as an excuse not to seriously consider the ideas which challenge their worldview. "The Dude" in the Coen Brothers film "The Big Lebowski" exemplifies this attitude.

Of course, Plato was very clear on the difference between knowledge and opinion. If all we can hold about subjects are opinions based on our own cultural biases which are just as valid as other people's opinions, then we are in trouble, and clearly, very few live their lives on such a basis. Anyway, relativism again falls foul of a self-inflicted undermining. If you can see the problem with this statement you will be aware of the irony: "There is no objective truth apart from the truth that there is no objective truth".

A study of Natural Law in the first year of the course will bring students face to face with an ethical belief-system based on the notion of objective truth revealed by reason. As students usually experience a tension between elements of this system and elements of the postmodern assumptions of contemporary culture, it is important to spend time looking at the philosophical underpinnings of both worldviews. One area where this can be interesting is to look at the institution of marriage from traditional and modern standpoints. Some of the key topics in this module are:

- Natural Law and Eternal Law

- The concept of Telos (purpose)

- The doctrine of Double Effect

- The possibility of Objective Moral Law and relation to subjective judgements

- The applicability of moral judgement to different areas of life

Then as a contrast a relativist, pragmatist approach to Christian ethics is introduced - Situation Ethics. Students get the chance to examine Fletcher's modern take on the Gospel value of agape, or Christian Love. Some key topics here include:

- How useful the concept of agape is

- Whether situation ethics can be said to be "Christian" or religious ethics

- Whether relativism, pragmatism, positivism and personalism are useful

How to use this book

The OCR Religious Studies AS offers a wide range of choice for the teacher and student to pick from. There are three one hour and fifteen minute exams: one Philosophy, one Ethics and one from a perspective of religious thought.

This book provides you with detailed summaries of all parts of the OCR AS Religious Studies Component 02 on religion and ethics specification.

We have put extra resources on our website which you can access by scanning the code at the end of the chapter with your smartphone. The website resources are also organised under the specification headings. The code will take you directly to the module you have scanned and you can browse between modules on the site. You will find Key Quotes, Practice Questions and more. If you are reading a Kindle version of this book, you can click on the link at the end of each chapter.

At the beginning of each chapter, you will find a list of key words and their definitions. Many of these key words are in **BOLD** in the text so that you can see them used in context. In places, other words are highlighted as prompts for you to remember the content.

Contents

Religious Approaches

Normative Ethical Theories

Applied Ethics

Religious Approaches

Natural Law

Situation Ethics

Natural Law

Natural Law is a **NORMATIVE** ethical theory. It has an underlying

TELEOLOGICAL orientation, and has its origins in the work of Aristotle, but was developed by Aquinas. In other words, a key assumption of Natural Law is that humans by their nature pursue certain **ENDS** which they perceive as good.

KEYWORDS

- **NATURAL LAW -** Normative, teleological ethical theory based on the work of Aristotle, that ethics is based on natural pursuit of rational ends

- **GOOD LIFE -** The belief that there is a rational goal to life, formulated by the ancient Greeks as a life of restraint and civic duty

- **ARISTOTELIAN -** Derived from the thought of Aristotle (384-322 BC)

- **TELOS** - Greek word meaning end or goal

- **TELEOLOGICAL -** Relating to an explanation of a thing in terms of its end or goal

- **MORALITY -** System of beliefs and practices relating to how one ought to live and behave towards others

- **ETERNAL LAW -** According to Aquinas, the law with which God governs the universe

- **DIVINE LAW -** The laws of God which have been revealed to humans, most notably on Mt. Sinai to Moses

- **HUMAN LAW -** Laws which have been derived from human reason alone

- **PRECEPTS -** A specific rule, usually derived from more general principles

- **AXIOM** - An assumption or working principle, not derived from previous arguments, but without which an argument may not be able to be proposed

- **ABSOLUTE -** Having an unchangeable character, not dependent on culture or time

- **RELATIVE/RELATIVISM -** Having a quality in relation to other things, and thus not absolute - time and culture dependent

- **POST-MODERN -** Describing system of thought in which there is no single story or "meta-narrative" about the world - thus relative

- **CONSTRUCTIVISM -** Belief that significant concepts such as number are constructs or human creations, and have no character or meaning beyond the context in which they were created

ORIGINS OF THE CONCEPT OF TELOS IN ARISTOTLE

The notion that the **GOOD LIFE** is one that conforms to the proper ends or goals of humans comes from Aristotle.

Further, that these ends can be discerned through rational reflection on human nature, is an **ARISTOTELIAN** claim.

The idea that **MORALITY** consists in fulfilling one's proper goals, or that the good life is one lived in accordance with our proper ends is a **TELEOLOGICAL** one (**TELOS-** goal or end).

AQUINAS AND NATURAL LAW

In the **SUMMA THEOLOGIAE**, Aquinas develops the notion of a natural law and brings it into a scriptural context, so that it fits with Christian theology. He puts it in the context of more universal laws:

- **ETERNAL LAW** - "The plan by which God, as ruler of the universe, governs all things". All things follow the eternal law in that they "have a tendency to pursue whatever behaviour and goals are appropriate to them".

- **LIMITED UNDERSTANDING** - Human beings, however, follow God's eternal law "in a more profound way". We have a limited understanding of the eternal law, and this means we can use our reason to find out what goals are appropriate for us to follow.

  This planning, both for ourselves and other creatures, is a way of sharing in God's plan. To participate in the eternal law in this way through reason is what Aquinas calls natural law.

- **NATURAL LAW** - The precepts of Natural Law (see below)

- **DIVINE LAW** - Laws revealed by God, for example, the **TEN COMMANDMENTS**, received by Moses on Mt. Sinai. Revealed in scripture, such laws are not necessarily capable of being arrived at by reason alone. They transcend rational discernment, although reason, when used correctly, is not at odds with divine law.

- **HUMAN LAW** - Laws arrived at by a process of rational argumentation, which can supplement the natural law, or specify in more detail what the natural law requires in specific circumstances. Human law should be in accordance with natural law, otherwise it deviates from law understood in its widest sense.

THE PRECEPTS OF NATURAL LAW

Aquinas builds his system of practical reasoning on certain fundamental principles.

One principle is that all practical reasoning depends on a notion of the good. Therefore a basic principle of moral reasoning is that **GOOD SHOULD BE DONE AND PURSUED AND EVIL AVOIDED**.

This is an axiom of **MORAL REASONING**, meaning that it is a self-evident starting point, and it is the key principle of natural law.

There are three **KEY SETS OF GOALS** which Aquinas identifies as good. From his perspective, good means whatever man naturally seeks as a goal.

With these three groups he works out some general moral principles, which are known as **THE PRECEPTS**:

- **GROUP 1** - The basic inclination to go on existing, which all things share, can be seen to be the basis of the moral principle to preserve life.

- **GROUP 2** - The natural tendency which humans and animals share to mate and bring up their young is the next moral principle.

- **GROUP 3** - Distinctively human ends, accessible through reason, are in this group. These are essentially to know the truth about God and to live in society, of which Aquinas gives instances, like shunning ignorance and not offending others.

Notice that these groups progress from general to specific, ie, from all life, to animal and human life, to just humans. This is in line with Aquinas' ideas about vegetative, animal and rational souls, which makes a similar progression.

These groups are often set out as **FIVE PRIMARY PRECEPTS**. These can be set out as:

- **PRESERVATION OF LIFE** - Group 1

- **REPRODUCTION** - Group 2

- **EDUCATION** - Group 2

- **LIVE IN AN ORDERED SOCIETY** - Group 3

- **WORSHIP GOD** - Group 3

The primary precepts can be memorised with the mnemonic **POWER** - **P**reservation, **O**rdered society, **W**orship, **E**ducation, **R**eproduction.

The Secondary Precepts

Each primary precept can be applied to specific situations to produce secondary precepts. These are not as absolute as the primary precepts, and only apply in **CERTAIN SITUATIONS**.

Examples are national laws, which may vary from country to country, eg. laws about marriage, or codes of behaviour that differ in different cultures. For instance, the laws regarding the age of consent or marriage can be as low as 13 in some countries and up to 18 in others. It is a crime in Singapore to chew gum, and heavy fines can be imposed for it, whereas elsewhere, it is not.

The secondary precepts are therefore **REALISTIC** and **FLEXIBLE**.

Apparent Goods

An apparent good is that which merely seems good to us; it satisfies a desire, and is an object of choice, but it is not a true good, as it actually goes against the whole purpose of a human being. Aquinas thinks no-one can seek an evil in and for itself, but everyone is pursuing what they believe is a good for themselves.

As our ultimate purpose is union with God, any good we pursue which ultimately frustrates that purpose cannot be a true good. This means that there are lesser goods, which, when we don't seek to elevate them above their own place, are not a problem. They only become problematic when, due to the disordered nature of our will, we give them undue importance in our lives.

IS NATURAL LAW A HELPFUL METHOD OF MORAL DECISION-MAKING?

Strengths

- **ABSOLUTE & RELATIVE** - It provides both absolute and relative precepts which could be helpful in a variety of situations

- **BASED ON REASON** - Therefore it is accessible to all humans

- **RELEVANT** - The precepts are timeless and relevant to modern society

- **FLEXIBLE** - The secondary precepts help give some flexibility to the system

Weaknesses

- **WHAT IS NATURAL?** - Difficulty deciding on what "natural" is, eg, doctors can prolong someone's life, but does that make it unnatural?

- **KARL BARTH** - A Protestant theologian who rejects use of reason. We should rely on revelation alone to know God's law

- **RELATIVISM CHALLENGE** - The challenge from relativism - does human nature alter over time/culture?

- **THERE IS NO 'NATURE'** - Postmodern/constructivist theory that humans project their own need for order or create narratives to impose order, but that there is none objectively

- **THERE IS NO 'TELOS'** - To the human or the natural world, evolution has dispensed with that idea. We give ourselves our purpose

---

NEED MORE HELP ON NATURAL LAW?

Use your phone to scan this QR code

Situation Ethics

There are ethical theories which claim that utilitarianism is a philosophical version of the Christian command to love your neighbour as yourself. Joseph Fletcher put forward one such theory in situation ethics.

It is a liberal Christian ethical theory

JOSEPH FLETCHER was an American Anglican. He wanted to avoid inflexible versions of Christian ethics which propose absolute rules. Equally he wanted to avoid the opposite extreme of "do what you will".

One way of seeing this is as taking the middle way between **ANTINOMIANISM** and **LEGALISM**.

The only absolute in situation ethics is the command to **LOVE YOUR NEIGHBOUR AS YOURSELF.**

Influenced by **TILLICH**, who said that God is the ground of our being (Tillich's term for God as the ultimate concern of humanity, or that he is more fundamental to our existence than anything else), God is immanent and therefore part of us, so we should not see morality as a set of orders from above, but as a moral law within.

Fletcher says:

> *"Love's decisions are not made prescriptively, but situationally".*

To love your neighbour means to consistently "will and choose the good of the other", in other words, to love what God loves, which is your neighbour's good. In that case we need only work out what will cause his or her good in the situation that he or she is in.

KEYWORDS

- **IMMANENT -** Within the world, in time and space

- **ANTINOMIANISM -** Belief that there are no moral laws that God expects Christians to obey - opposite to legalism

- **LEGALISM -** Belief that obedience to religious law earns salvation

- **AGAPE -** Greek word often translated as Christian or brotherly love

- **PRESCRIPTIVE -** Giving rules or instructions

- **PRAGMATISM -** Belief that a key aspect of truth is if it is productive of positive results, that the meaning of a proposition is found in the practical consequences of accepting it

- **POSITIVISM -** Any system that confines itself to experience and excludes metaphysical theories

- **PERSONALISM -** Belief that the person is central to ethics - and therefore rules/legalism are secondary

- **PAPAL ENCYCLICAL** - A category of letter sent by the Pope to the Catholic faithful

AGAPE

Greek word in new testament meaning **LOVE OF NEIGHBOUR**, deriving from Old Testament Hebrew word **CHESED** meaning mercy

Agape is often translated as Christian love or BROTHERLY LOVE.

New Testament passages which speak of it: **1 JOHN 4:16,21**

> *"God is love. Whoever lives in love lives in God, and God in them. And he has given us this command: Anyone who loves God must also love their brother and sister".*

Agape is embodied in the person of Jesus Christ ("The Word became flesh and dwelt among us")

THE SIX PROPOSITIONS

These give rise to the theory of situation ethics and are fundamental principles focused on the nature of **LOVE** or AGAPE

Situation ethics is a working out of the consequences of these principles, according to Fletcher:

LOVE ...

1. **IS INTRINSICALLY GOOD** - Agape is not about being, but doing; goodness lies in the consequences. Fletcher says you cannot assign good or bad to actions

2. **IS THE RULING NORM -** In ethical decision-making, love is the ruling norm and replaces all laws. Essentially, Fletcher is saying

that **LOVE IS THE LAW**, in the sense that love replaces all laws. So nothing, not even murder, is intrinsically bad if it leads to the most loving outcome

3. **LOVE & JUSTICE ARE THE SAME THING** - Justice is love that is **DISTRIBUTED**. If love is put into practice, it will result in justice. You cannot love someone and allow them to be discriminated against

4. **IS EQUAL** - Love wills the neighbour's good regardless of whether the neighbour is liked or not. There is no favouritism in love, all must be treated equally, even one's enemies. This means we are bound to love others as much as our families

5. **IS ULTIMATE** - Love is the goal or end of the act and that justifies any means to achieve that goal. Love must be the final end of an act, rather than the means to some other goal; we must not be loving to achieve something else

6. **IS SITUATIONAL** - Love decides on each situation as it arises without a set of laws to guide it. Love is therefore situational, not prescriptive; there will not be one set of moral guidelines which covers all situations, but the right thing to do in each situation will be the most loving. This makes it **RELATIVISTIC**

THE FOUR WORKING PRINCIPLES

As well as six propositions about love, Fletcher also gives **FOUR WORKING PRINCIPLES**. Whereas the six propositions were about the nature of love and the consequences for the ethical theory, the four working principles are structural guidelines which situate the system within a wider conceptual framework.

1. **PRAGMATISM** - It is based on experience rather than theory. This is important because Fletcher wants to get away from legalism which can seem remote to people's lived experience. One way of rephrasing pragmatism is "whatever works is the best thing to do". In the context of ethics, this means the best thing to do will be the pathway that produces the most loving outcome.

2. **RELATIVISM** - It is based on making the absolute laws of Christian ethics relative. Everything must be relative to agape, so there is no such thing as a command to "never do" a certain action. **REJECTS TEN COMMANDMENTS**. Notice that agape is absolute, but must be relativised to every situation.

3. **POSITIVISM** - It begins with belief in the reality and importance of love. You have to begin with a positive choice or commitment to love. This is a value judgement, a saying yes to love. Why? Because God is Love. It expresses a belief that love is a feature of the universe.

4. **PERSONALISM** - Persons, not laws or anything else, are at the centre of situation ethics. Similar to Kant's maxim 'treat people as ends, never as means to an end'. Laws take second place to

people. God is personal, and wants a personal relationship with us.

Strengths

- **PRAGMATIC** - Many who work in pastoral areas are grateful for an ethical system which can actually be applied to the person in front of them, rather than a set of rules which may not be suitable for that person.

- **LOVE IS CENTRAL** - As it is in the Gospel. This is an essential aspect of situation ethics, which does conform to the greatest commandments as given by Jesus.

- **RELATIVE MEANS FLEXIBLE** - Again, those who work pastorally need a certain flexibility to help them set the person on a pathway back to God - this is often expressed as "meeting people where they are".

Weaknesses

- **'WHATEVER WORKS' IS MORALLY DUBIOUS**- Does pragmatism dispense truth for utility? In other words, as long as I say the right things and act in ways which bring about the most 'loving outcome', then my action is above criticism. But this is to forget that morality has a prescriptive element - value judgements have to be made, in particular the value judgement that can tell what is loving or not.

- **'PERSONS VS RULES' IS FALSE** - Does personalism, in

privileging people over laws, create a false dichotomy which risks affirming people in whatever course of action they may be on, regardless of whether it is objectively sinful or not?

CONSCIENCE

According to **FLETCHER**, conscience is not a noun but a verb, a term that describes attempts to make decisions creatively. Fletcher is interested in the reality of love in action and conscience really describes the process of **PUTTING LOVE INTO ACTION**, of willing the good of another.

Fletcher rejects the idea that conscience is intuition, a channel for divine guidance (the voice of God idea), the internalised values of the individual's culture (famously put forward by **FREUD**), or the part of reason that makes value judgements, because all of these try to treat conscience as a thing rather than the process of making decisions creatively.

The Catholic Church rejected situation ethics, not least for the radical departure it makes from the traditional notion of conscience. In the **PAPAL ENCYCLICAL** Veritatis Splendor (1993) Pope John Paul II said:

"The relationship between man's freedom and God's law is most deeply lived out in the "heart" of the person, in his moral conscience. As the Second Vatican Council observed: "In the depths of his conscience man detects a law which he does not impose on himself, but which holds him to obedience. Always summoning him to love good and avoid evil, the voice of conscience can when necessary speak to his heart more specifically: 'do this, shun that'. For man has in his heart a law written by God. To obey it is the very dignity of man; according to it he will be judged (cf. Rom 2:14-16)".

"The way in which one conceives the relationship between freedom and law is thus intimately bound up with one's understanding of the moral conscience. Here the cultural tendencies referred to above - in which freedom and law are set in opposition to each other and kept apart, and freedom is exalted almost to the point of idolatry - lead to a "creative" understanding of moral conscience, which diverges from the teaching of the Church's tradition and her Magisterium."

IS SITUATION ETHICS CAPABLE OF GIVING REAL MORAL GUIDANCE?

Strengths

- **INDIVIDUAL** - Avoids problem of overly rigid inflexible "dogmatic" moral systems which sometimes fail to account for individual situations.

- **FLEXIBLE** - Deontological theories such as Kantian ethics prescribe universal rules which common sense tells us are occasionally inapplicable - situation ethics deals easily with these dilemmas (such as "is it ok to lie sometimes"?).

- **ATTRACTIVE** - Many modern Christians, especially those who work in pastoral areas who need practical applications of Christian ethics which are flexible, find this attractive.

Weaknesses

- **OUTDATED** - Many Christian ethicists regard situation ethics as not having aged well - it is very much from the era of free love and hippies.

- **WEAKNESSES OF CONSEQUENTIALISM** - As it is essentially a form of act-utilitarianism, it suffers from most of the same problems.

- **IT IS TOO THIN** - Lacks a coherent account of the fulness of

Christian ethics, and attempts to use a secular philosophical theory to explain a Christian theological system. Some would say it fails to do this adequately.

- **TOO VAGUE** - People need rules to live by.

- **SKIN DEEP** - Despite what Fletcher claims, situation ethics is essentially antinomianism with a veneer of agape to make it palatable to Christians.

- **IMPULSIVE** - Situations do not exist outside of the people in them, who will have their own unconscious or conscious value system which they bring to it. Situation ethics does not stop people acting on impulses or poorly considered values and then retrospectively fitting their actions into an **AGAPEISTIC** framework.

- **UNCERTAINTY** - How can we always know what the most loving thing to do will be? **CHILDRESS** says:

"We cannot say which acts are right or wrong, what we ought to do, until we can say which will probably produce more good than evil but we cannot say which will probably produce more good than evil until we have some conception of value. Situation ethics gives us no help there"

NEED MORE HELP ON SITUATION ETHICS?

Use your phone to scan this QR code

Normative Ethical Theories

Kant

Utilitarianism

Kantian Ethics

IMMANUEL KANT (1724-1804) was a profoundly influential German philosopher who wrote extensively on ethics. His theory is **DEONTOLOGICAL**, meaning it is concerned with duty, and is absolutist.

KEYWORDS

- **DEONTOLOGICAL** - Ethical system based on deon - Greek for duty - judges morality of action based on whether it has followed rules

- **DIVINE COMMAND THEORY** - System of morality in which morality is divinely revealed, without need for human reason

- **EPISTEMOLOGY** - Theory of knowledge, or study of foundations of how we know

- **NOUMENAL** - Kantian term for world unattainable by human experience - mind-independent

- **PHENOMENAL** - Opposite of noumenal - anything which can be apprehended by senses

- **GOOD WILL** - Faculty of acting according to a conception of law - "the only thing good without limitation" according to Kant

- **HYPOTHETICAL IMPERATIVE** - Any action based on desires, so reason commands it only if it is desired

- **CATEGORICAL IMPERATIVE** - Any action which must be done for its own sake, regardless of whether it is an object of desire

- **CONDITIONAL** - Dependent on factors which might not apply in all cases

- **MAXIM** - A general law or rule of action, often stated in a simple sentence

- **POSTULATE** - A statement accepted as true for the purposes of argument

- **IMMORTALITY** - Inability to die, or ability to live forever

- **SUMMUM BONUM** - The highest good

BACKGROUND TO KANT'S ETHICAL THEORY

Kant's ethics should be understood in the light of his **EPISTEMOLOGY**. He believed that it was impossible to have direct knowledge of God, and thus we could not know what was right and wrong through God's commands, as **DIVINE COMMAND THEORY** would claim.

Equally, we cannot know what is right or wrong though looking at the consequences of an action, as utilitarian theories would claim. This is because all **CONSEQUENCES** belong to the world of experience, what Kant calls the **PHENOMENAL REALM**, and you cannot discover moral value within this realm. For Kant, **MORALITY** is part of the **NOUMENAL REALM**, or the world of reason. Experience, the phenomenal realm, can tell you what to do if you require a certain outcome, but not the things that you should be aiming for - that is the job of **REASON** in the noumenal world.

These two, the **HYPOTHETICAL** and **CATEGORICAL IMPERATIVES**, form the basis of Kant's ethical theory.

There is therefore a moral code which can be known through reason, and it is based on duty. This can be defined as acting morally according to the good regardless of the consequences. You should do something because it is the right thing to do. If something is the right thing to do it is right irrespective of time or place or situation.

Kant says that the only thing that can be said to be good without exception is a **GOOD WILL**. Many other things will be good in certain situations, but only a good will will be good in all. For instance, self-control is good, but can be used by evil people to make their evil deeds more effective.

The idea of a good will is a critical aspect of Kant's moral theory.

THE HYPOTHETICAL IMPERATIVE

Therefore, the hypothetical imperative, as previously discussed is simply what you do if you require a certain outcome (a command to act to achieve a certain result).

For instance, someone might say that you should study under a certain tutor, and read certain books, or use certain tools, if you want to be a good wood engraver. This might be a command because the person giving it wants you to be the best wood engraver, but it is not a moral command.

Equally, someone might require you to wear a certain uniform if you want to go to a specific school. This again is an **IMPERATIVE TO ACT** in a certain way if you want a specific thing. Notice that there is a conditional sense to these commands, "'if you want something, you should do this", rather than simply, "you should do this, no matter what". This would be a categorical imperative.

THE CATEGORICAL IMPERATIVE

This is simply a command to act that is good in itself regardless of consequences. It is the imperative of morality because it can be deduced through reason and universalised.

It can be formulated in three ways:

1. **FORMULA OF THE LAW OF NATURE** - Whereby a maxim can be established as a universal law. Kant says:

    "Act only on that maxim through which you can at the same time will that it should become a universal law".

    An example might be obtaining a loan by making a false promise. If everybody did this, no one would believe such promises. Therefore this maxim contradicts itself. Only maxims which can be universalised without contradiction are valid.

2. **FORMULA OF THE END IN ITSELF** - Whereby people are treated as ends in themselves, not as means to an end. Kant says:

    "Act in such a way that you always treat humanity, whether in your own person or in the person of any other, never simply as a means, but always at the same time as an end".

    This means we should treat people with respect, and not use them to further our own goals. If we don't do this we undermine their status as rational agents.

3. **FORMULA OF THE KINGDOM OF ENDS** - Whereby a society of rationality is established in which people treat each other as ends and not means. Kant says:

"Every rational being must so act as if he were through his maxims a law-making member in the universal kingdom of ends."

Kant thinks that one's own reason ought to be able to tell one if something is immoral. For example, obtaining a loan using a false promise cannot be universalised; one's own reason can tell one something that is universally valid, so all other members of a society should be reaching the same conclusions about the maxims.

THE THREE POSTULATES

They are:

1. **FREEDOM**

2. **IMMORTALITY**

3. **GOD**

The postulates are **IMPLICIT ASSUMPTIONS** which according to Kant, every time you act morally you are accepting.

Why?

To act morally you must be free

You must have the ability to freely use your reason to work out the right thing to do; if you are compelled to act in the "right" way your action is not a moral one, because you had no choice in it.

Why should we need immortality then?

Doing the right thing should be crowned with happiness

Kant calls this the **SUMMUM BONUM**.

But it is unusual that doing the right thing makes us happy in this life, therefore, there needs to be a further existence after death in which we can attain the summum bonum.

And of course, if there is an afterlife, there needs to be a God to provide that and to crown us with the summum bonum.

IS NATURAL LAW A HELPFUL METHOD OF MORAL DECISION-MAKING?

Strengths

- **INFLUENTIAL** - It has been highly influential on ethical thought.

- **COHERENT** - It builds a coherent and detailed system, which can deal with many different ethical situations.

- **HARD TO DENY** - Key insights of the theory are hard to deny: it is clear that morality cannot derive from experience alone, or to put it another way, you cannot get an **OUGHT** from an **IS.**

- **STRONGER THAN RELATIVIST THEORIES** - Has none of the weaknesses of relativist theories. There are universal moral absolutes which can be known through reason. This is very clearly the basis of much of the thinking from the Enlightenment, and modern societies and democracies mainly implicitly accept this.

Weaknesses

- **ONLY A THEORY** - It is only a formal theory, which gives no practical guidelines for particular situations. This is very good if you want an account of what morality is, but less helpful if you want to know how to act morally.

- **UNTRIED** - A response to this is that Kant never tries in the Groundwork of the Metaphysic of Morals to lay out practical guidelines - he does this elsewhere.

- **SUSPICIOUS** - Are any actions free from ulterior motives? Can we ever do something purely out of duty?

- **UNEMOTIONAL** - There is little room for emotion or feeling in the system, and yet for many people morality is intimately involved with feeling. For example, I may be moved out of pity to help another. Even Christ at times seemed to be moved in this way before he acted.

- **INFLEXIBLE** - The system seems to be too inflexible, and could give rise to rules which are too rigid or even silly, for instance, the famous example of not lying to the axe-murderer.

NEED MORE HELP ON KANTIAN ETHICS?

Use your phone to scan this QR code

Utilitarianism

Utilitarianism is a **TELEOLOGICAL** ethical theory which employs the concept of utility in a relativist approach. Utility could be defined as seeking the greatest balance of good over evil, or pleasure over pain.

Utilitarianism was first propounded by **JEREMY BENTHAM** in 1789.

The **PRINCIPLE OF UTILITY** is simply that the best consequences should be brought about from any action.

It is a **CONSEQUENTIALIST** theory which defines the right action as one that will bring about the greatest good.

A simple slogan for utilitarian theories might be **THE END JUSTIFIES THE MEANS**.

KEYWORDS

- **UTILITY** - Key principle of Utilitarianism - criterion of usefulness of an action

- **CONSEQUENTIALISM** - Moral system in which the results or consequences of an action are key to deciding its value

- **HEDONIC CALCULUS** - System invented by Jeremy Bentham in which pleasure and pain are weighed against each other to decide on whether a course of action should be pursued

- **QUANTITATIVE** - Relating to quantity

- **QUALITATIVE** - Relating to quality

- **HIERARCHY** - System of sacred order, in which the greater quality is placed above that of greater quantity

- **TYRANNY OF THE MAJORITY** - Term to describe the imposition of the wishes of the many over the wishes of the few

- **SELF-EVIDENT** - Inherently obvious, clear from the description

- **NATURALISTIC FALLACY** - Error of reasoning in which an "is" is derived from an "ought" - eg, feeling jealous is only natural, therefore there is nothing wrong with feeling jealous

THE HEDONIC CALCULUS

It is calculating the **BENEFIT** or **HARM** of an act through its consequences. When a utilitarian wants to know what will produce the greatest happiness they need to do a calculation or measurement.

How do you measure happiness? Bentham proposed the **HEDONIC CALCULUS** which quantified pleasure using seven measures:

1. **INTENSITY** - If pleasure lacks intensity its value decreases on the scale

2. **DURATION -** If the pleasure is short-lived its value is lower

3. **CERTAINTY** or **UNCERTAINTY -** How likely is the action to cause pleasure?

4. **PROPINQUITY** - Also means nearness or remoteness

5. **FECUNDITY** - The likelihood of its being followed by other similar sensations

6. **PURITY** - The likelihood of its not being followed by opposite: painful sensations

7. **EXTENT** - The number of people affected by it

ACT UTILITARIANISM

Proposed by **JEREMY BENTHAM**, Act Utilitarianism was the original form of the theory, and is viewed by many as less sophisticated than later versions. Jeremy Bentham was born into a wealthy family in 1748 and died in 1842. His body has been preserved and is in a glass display case in University College London.

ACT UTILITARIANISM is focused on individual situations and particular actions, thus - the act. Bentham was influenced by Locke and Hume, and his empiricist and analytical approach led him to focus on actions which he believed could be given a quantitative value and weighed against the value of other actions to decide on the best course of action.

It is a relative ethical theory; as in all consequentialist theories, the assumption is that what is right will vary from situation to situation. There is also a moral and psychological individualism to the theory - for Bentham the self is the fundamental unit, and there is no real other unit such as society or the church etc. This means that what is pleasurable or painful to the individual is to be given supreme importance in deciding on actions.

This individualism is a result of the emphasis on human reasoning in the Enlightenment. Duncan and Gray say that for Bentham:

> *"The individual human being is conceived as the source of values and as himself the supreme value." (Duncan, Graeme & Gray, John. "The Left Against Mill," in New Essays on John Stuart Mill and Utilitarianism, Eds. Wesley E. Cooper, Kai Nielsen and Steven C. Patten, 1979.)*

Bentham's theory is also quantitative - the hedonic calculus reduces happiness to a quantity worked out through an equation. This strikes many as rather odd, and in practice extremely difficult to do.

The theory is based on pleasure, thus hedonistic - Bentham takes it that the principle thing individuals do is to avoid pain and seek pleasure. This view of human nature has been contested by many before and after. For instance, Plato thinks that when humans know what is good for them they will seek that good, even if it doesn't immediately satisfy any hedonic calculus.

Ultimately act utilitarianism follows one principle - the **PRINCIPLE OF UTILITY** - and that must be adhered to. But the principle, that the best consequences should be brought out of any action, is not rich enough to provide sufficient moral guidance.

RULE UTILITARIANISM

Proposed by **JOHN STUART MILL,** rule utilitarianism is a later theory which significantly modified Bentham's earlier work. In broadening and giving a more sophisticated account of happiness, Mill manages to create a moral theory which has some value.

Instead of happiness as pleasure, Mill focuses on happiness in a broader sense. This is quite an obvious move, as the study of happiness by many philosophers throughout the ages has yielded a vast amount of thought as to what happiness is. It was quite simple for Mill to expand the definition of happiness into a hierarchical scheme.

The key thing that Mill does here is to identify and distinguish between **HIGHER PLEASURES** and **LOWER PLEASURES**. Some examples might be: eating a cream cake is a lower pleasure compared to learning to play an instrument; making money is a lower pleasure than using that money to fund philanthropic ventures.

There is also a difference in Mill's principle of utility: Happiness is desirable. Happiness is the only thing desirable as an end in itself – the general happiness of all is desirable. Increasing the happiness of others increases your own. Psychological studies have recently shown this to be true - reducing happiness to seeking pleasure and avoiding pain does not do justice to the complexity of the human search for happiness.

Mill had general rules which were applied universally across societies to promote happiness, thus his theory is not quantitative or relativist like act utilitarianism. It could be said to be qualitative in that it looks at higher and lower pleasures, and judges some as intrinsically more valuable than others.

IS UTILITARIANISM A HELPFUL METHOD OF MORAL DECISION-MAKING?

Strengths

- **JUSTIFIED** - Mill addresses the problem of justifying the principle of utility with some degree of success.

- **HAPPINESS RULES** - He acknowledges that it cannot be proved but points out that happiness is the only thing desirable as an end in itself, and that everything we do is usually done for its sake.

- **GREATEST HAPPINESS PRINCIPLE** - Therefore, as everything we do is either a form of happiness or a means to happiness, the greatest happiness principle can be accepted as a fundamental principle of morality, as it is in line with the ultimate goal to which we direct our lives.

- **ATTRACTIVE SIMPLICITY** - Bentham's system has an attractive simplicity, which (if it worked!) would count towards its usefulness as a moral theory.

Weaknesses

▶ **Mill's problems with Bentham's theory**

■ **UNQUANTIFIABLE** - How is it possible to quantify happiness? Can this be done when faced with an ethical dilemma? Can it be done at all?

■ **HARD TO PREDICT** - Problems with the teleological nature of Bentham's theory, it is hard to predict what the consequences will always be of an action.

■ **TOO SUBJECTIVE** - What is pleasure? It is too subjective. Some people take pleasure in things that others find painful or repulsive.

■ **NO HIERARCHY** - It does not distinguish between different sorts of pleasures. There is no attempt at hierarchy; surely there are nobler and cruder pleasures? Some pleasures are surely little more than animal instincts.

■ **TYRANNY OF THE MAJORITY** - Emphasis on greatest good for greatest number leads to a tyranny of the majority. What about the needs of the minority?

▶ **Other problems**

■ **UNJUSTIFIABLE** - How does Bentham justify his principle of utility? He says it does not have to be proved as it is like the first principle of an argument, a self-evident truth.

■ **NOT DERIVED FROM HAPPINESS** - Some have noted that

Bentham does seem to derive his principle of utility from the observation that the desire for happiness is fundamental to all humans.

- **NATURALISTIC FALLACY** - This would be a case of committing the naturalistic fallacy, of deriving an **IS** from an **OUGHT**.

- **NO MORAL CURRENCY** - Pleasure varies dramatically and it is not clear that all human goals can be expressed in it; for instance, if one person gains deep pleasure from watching another person succeeding at a task, or from helping someone to become well, whilst another person gains pleasure from torturing innocent people or from bingeing on alcohol, then it is difficult to make the notion of pleasure a unit of moral currency.

- **UNWORKABLE** - Mill's richer account of pleasure makes the hedonic calculus unworkable.

NEED MORE HELP ON UTILITARIANISM?

Use your phone to scan this QR code

Applied Ethics

Euthanasia

Business Ethics

Euthanasia

The topic of euthanasia raises important moral questions which can be answered in different ways by different moral theories. This section highlights the main issues.

KEYWORDS

- **EUTHANASIA** - "Gentle or easy death" - helping those who are suffering to die

- **SANCTITY OF LIFE** - Christian notion that human life is intrinsically valuable as a creation of God

- **DIGNITY** - Worthy of respect, having intrinsic value as human

- **AUTONOMY** - Controlled by self, rather than another - independence

- **POST-ENLIGHTENMENT** - After the 17th Century philosophical movement which championed reason

- **SLIPPERY SLOPE** - Type of argument in which it is assumed that if certain things are permitted, other more destructive things will follow as a result

WHAT IS EUTHANASIA?

The term could be translated as **GOOD DEATH**; euthanasia is usually seen as killing someone else whose life is not thought worth living.

There is a distinction between active and passive euthanasia:

- **ACTIVE** - Doing something to bring about or hasten the death of the person, such as administering a lethal dose of a drug.

- **PASSIVE** - Causing or hastening death by omitting to do something, or ceasing to provide something that was needed for life to continue. This might be something such as removing feeding tubes.

SANCTITY OF LIFE

Sanctity of life is a notion with roots in the Judaeo-Christian tradition. It is an articulation of an absolute value or intrinsic worth to all human life based on the idea of life as a **GIFT FROM GOD**, the creator of all things, and the particular position of man as the pinnacle of creation on the sixth day, being made in the image and likeness of God.

In **GENESIS**, God creates all things and sees that they are "very good". Created things are dependent on God for their existence. However, their goodness is not simply part of God's substance but is an independent result of their being **GIFTED** their existence by God.

This means that we should value and cherish all life, and particularly human life.

If God is the real owner of all life then we do not have the right to dispose of it as we will - there are limits to what we can do with it.

Therefore, sanctity of life denotes an **UNCONDITIONAL** value to all human life, regardless of age, mental or physical capacity.

In the Encyclical Evangelium vitae, Pope John Paul II draws on the Christian tradition to make the case that suicide is "as morally objectionable as murder". Equally, the Catholic church sees euthanasia - helping someone to commit suicide - as objectionable for the same reasons.

QUALITY OF LIFE

Quality of life arguments are usually set in contrast to sanctity of life arguments, as they emphasise the importance of the capacity of the human person to lead a life in which some level of personal flourishing can occur, or that life should possess certain attributes to be worth living.

Usually, if a very low level of quality of life can be shown, ie. that the person experiences no remittance from constant intense suffering, and is severely incapacitated, then it is argued that the person should not be forced to continue to live against their own wishes.

The concept of quality of life has its origins in secular ideas of human freedom, dignity and autonomy, ideas which clearly are not alien to religious traditions, but which have been developed in different directions by post-enlightenment thinkers.

VOLUNTARY EUTHANASIA

Voluntary euthanasia is done at the request or with the consent of the person wishing to be killed. Voluntary euthanasia and assisted suicide are illegal in Britain, but are legal in the Netherlands and Belgium.

NON-VOLUNTARY EUTHANASIA

Non-voluntary euthanasia is done without the request or consent of the person who is killed. This is because the person is unable to give their consent, due to being in a persistent vegetative state (PVS), or for other reasons such as they are a very severely disabled newborn, or they have advanced Alzheimer's disease.

APPLICATION OF NATURAL LAW TO EUTHANASIA

The Catholic Church has taken a broadly natural law approach to euthanasia. In the thirteenth century Thomas Aquinas took suicide to be wrong because:

- **CONTRARY** - It is contrary to the natural law

- **HARMFUL** - It harms the human community to which the person belongs

- **WRONGFUL TO GOD** - It wrongs God whose gift life is and who alone has power over life and death

The Church has essentially applied this to euthanasia. Euthanasia goes against one of the primary precepts of natural law: to preserve life.

It also goes against the precept to live in an ordered society, as it could be seen as introducing harm and distress into the human community.

For instance, there are very strict rules on the reporting of suicide in the media in the UK, as there is a danger of encouraging impressionable people to do it, which academics argue was the case with the spate of suicides in Bridgend in Wales.

However, the doctrine of double effect, which is a key part of natural law, makes the case that as long as you do not intend to do evil, but to do good, it is acceptable to perform an action that may have the foreseen but unintended side-effect of causing an evil, as long as the evil side-effect is outweighed by the good intention.

This is applicable to euthanasia because large doses of pain-relieving drugs are often given which can have the side-effect of hastening the end of life of a patient – this would be an acceptable approach of natural law.

APPLICATION OF SITUATION ETHICS TO EUTHANASIA

The situationist just has to ask what the most loving thing to do in the situation would be. Clearly, many would argue that it is to help the person to end their suffering. However, some would argue that even if that was the most loving thing to do for the patient, it might not be the most loving thing to do for the loved ones.

For example, **SIMON BINNER** went to a Swiss euthanasia clinic to end his life after suffering from Motor Neurone Disease. In a documentary, his wife said that whilst respecting his decision, she felt he had deprived her and his family of the opportunity to care for him and nurse him through his final days.

A situationist would have to weigh up the different features of each element of this case. It is hard to see how a conclusion could be reached about what the most loving thing to do here is.

EVALUATION OF APPLIED ETHICAL THEORIES TO EUTHANASIA

Some would argue there is no rational basis for placing an **ABSOLUTE VALUE** on life in the way that sanctity of life arguments do:

- **WEAKNESS** - Firstly, from a secular viewpoint, scriptural or religious foundations for notions are seen as weak, because they simply do not have any more authority than a story.

  Therefore, to say that life has value because God created it carries little weight if you don't believe in God. However, some secular atheists do argue that life has an intrinsic value simply as human life.

- **OPENNESS TO DEATH** - Secondly, there are some religious viewpoints which point out that to seek to avoid death at all costs goes against the heart of what many religions preach, which is an openness to death.

In Christian traditions, martyrs have been honoured as those who die at the hand of those who hate the faith. But these people have not sought martyrdom, and therefore there can hardly be a comparison to ending life through euthanasia.

HUME pointed out that if there are limits on what I can do with my life as a loan from God, then they should apply not only to artificially ending my life, but to artificially prolonging my life through medicine etc.

UTILITARIAN approaches are also problematic; as we have seen, it might be hard to weigh the different needs of different people in the situation.

However, **PETER SINGER** argues that, in seeking to satisfy the preferences of all concerned, we can come to a coherent decision about suicide and euthanasia. If someone experiences their life as a terrible burden, to permit euthanasia could come close to satisfying the preferences of the ill person and their loved ones.

CONSEQUENTIALIST arguments can contribute to a **SLIPPERY SLOPE** argument against euthanasia. Examples usually point to the consequences on the old or infirm of legal euthanasia putting pressure on them to end their lives.

NEED MORE HELP ON EUTHANASIA?

Use your phone to scan this QR code

Business Ethics

"Being good is good business"

Anita Roddick

"A business that makes nothing but money is a poor kind of business"

Henry Ford

The ethical responsibility of companies, as well as larger questions about the ethical dimension of economics are discussed in this section.

KEYWORDS

- **CORPORATE SOCIAL RESPONSIBILITY** - A company's initiatives to take responsibility for their effect on environmental and social wellbeing

- **SHAREHOLDER** - Any person that owns at least one share of a company's stock

- **FLOURISHING** - State of personal fulfillment in which one's natural capacities are developed and practiced for the benefit of oneself and others

- **WEALTH** - Riches, monetary or otherwise

- **STAKEHOLDERS** - Anyone with a stake in a company, either internal or external, eg. a customer or employer

- **WHISTLE-BLOWING** - The practice of revealing dubious or unethical practices at a corporation by an employee

- **GLOBALISATION** - Gradual homogenisation of markets in different countries due to increased ease of communication and travel

- **FAIR TRADE** - Ethically based initiative which aims to give local producers a fair wage in a multinational system which often results in injustice and inequality due to maximum profit being sought

- **ENNUI** - State of boredom or listlessness resulting from lack of meaning or significance to life

- **CAPITALISM -** Economic system based on private ownership.

- **CONSUMERISM** - Culture in which everything has a price, ideology which encourages consumption

- **DISTRIBUTISM** - Economic ideology based on the principles of Catholic Social Teaching

- **CAPITAL** - Any non-financial asset that is used in production of goods or services

- **EQUITABLE** - Fair and equal

- **SUBSIDIARITY** - An organising principle that matters ought to be handled by the smallest, lowest or least centralised competent authority

- **SOLIDARITY** - A firm and persevering determination to devote oneself to the common good

CORPORATE SOCIAL RESPONSIBILITY

Businesses have a **DUTY** and a **RESPONSIBILITY** to consider the effects of their activities on communities and the environment. When a company monitors its activities and ensures that it complies with the law as well as ethical norms, this is called **CORPORATE SOCIAL RESPONSIBILITY** (CSR).

The fundamental aim of a business could be framed in terms of making a profit. If this key aim of shareholders is allowed to override all other considerations then it becomes a matter of **ETHICAL CONCERN**.

A broader formulation of the aim of a business could be to generate wealth. Wealth is something that can be considered in purely monetary terms, but also in terms of human flourishing. If a business succeeds at generating these different forms of wealth it could be seen as an ethically responsible business.

This approach is often phrased as **GOOD ETHICS IS GOOD BUSINESS**; below are some examples of the interrelationship between these areas:

- **WORKERS** - For instance, a business might look after its workers and train them, provide opportunities for professional development and so on; this is good business sense because happy workers are productive workers.

- **ENVIRONMENT** - A company may get involved in local environmental schemes, such as tree-planting etc; this would not only offset any negative impact their **CARBON FOOTPRINT** makes, but also provide opportunities for a positive profile in the local area, and thus encourage more people to do business with them.

However, some would disagree with the broad formulation of the aim of a business to generate wealth not only in monetary terms.

For example, **MILTON FRIEDMAN** (1912-2006) an American economist, said that a business's social responsibility lies purely in increasing its profits, and that as long as it stays within the rules of the game, it should be able to freely engage in competition with a view to doing simply this.

INTERNAL & EXTERNAL STAKEHOLDERS

The idea of the corporate social responsibility of a business means that a business is obliged to consider different stakeholders. There are two types:

- **INTERNAL STAKEHOLDERS** - These are owners, managers, workers and suppliers, who respectively, are interested in; making a profit, earning a salary, keeping their jobs and earning high wages, and continuing to supply businesses with their products.

- **EXTERNAL STAKEHOLDERS** - These are customers, the local community and the local environment; these different groups have an interest in being able to buy good quality products at reasonable prices, having a reliable employer to keep local people in work, and wanting a business to impact positively on their environment, without air or noise pollution.

What kind of responsibility companies have to internal and external stakeholders will be the job of ethical theories to decide.

WHISTLE-BLOWING

The relationship between employer and employee is complex. This relationship is defined in law by a contract. There are also ethical considerations to be made in certain circumstances. For instance if an employee witnesses or learns of wrongdoing on the part of the employer, should they disclose this to others or the public? This is called **WHISTLE-BLOWING**.

Whistle-blowing raises questions of confidentiality and loyalty. How does an employee decide what it is in the public interest to know about the company?

Most would agree that it is easier to argue for whistle-blowing if there are issues of safety or financial misdemeanours at stake. With the advent of the internet it is now very easy for individuals to disseminate information about companies widely and there are several websites that exist to protect whistle-blowers.

GLOBALISATION

Globalisation refers to the fact that around the world economies, industries, markets, cultures and policy-making are becoming increasingly **MORE INTEGRATED**. Essentially, the differences between one economy and another are reduced, so that trade all over the world becomes increasingly similar.

Globalisation has increased in recent times for various reasons such as:

- **TRANSPORT** - Has become speedier and less costly

- **TECHNOLOGICAL CHANGE** - The internet and global communication have meant faster exchange of information

- **EMERGING MARKETS** - Developing countries provide new opportunities

- **FREE TRADE** - The removal of trade barriers, for instance, the EU

Some ethical issues related to globalisation are:

- **CHEAP LABOUR** - Companies are now freer to base themselves in countries where labour is cheap to reduce manufacturing costs. This can lead to **SWEAT SHOPS** and child workers.

- **FAIR TRADE** - Trade between countries can be unfair, with rich countries having very strong trade barriers.

- **CULTURAL EROSION** - As one-world markets emerge, the danger is that consumer culture begins to replace individual and cultural identities, with the loss of ancient traditions and the homogenisation of ways of living.

KANTIAN APPROACHES TO BUSINESS ETHICS

MILTON FRIEDMAN's standpoint, that a business's only responsibility is to its shareholders, would be disputed by Kant, who believed that people should not be used as a means to an end. If the workers are simply used as a means to make a profit, this goes against one of the basic tenets of Kantian ethics. Kantian ethics considers all stakeholders as worthy of consideration, and the owner of the business should act as a law-making member of a **KINGDOM OF ENDS**.

In terms of whistle-blowing, Kantian ethics considers what it is your duty to do. Your duty overrides any loyalty you might feel towards the company. If the safety of workers is at stake, you have a duty to protect them by blowing the whistle, regardless of whether it will cause you to lose your job.

UTILITARIAN APPROACHES TO BUSINESS ETHICS

In seeking to promote the **GREATEST GOOD** of the **GREATEST NUMBER**, utilitarianism would seem to be favourable to the workers, who outnumber the managers in business. Utilitarianism would stress the importance of workers' rights, and indeed, most forms of socialism and communism would have a utilitarian background.

However, utilitarian arguments might promote questionable business practices, as long as those practices favoured the greatest good of the greatest number.

For instance, if a local area was to be blighted by a factory, but many people would gain from the job opportunities it brought to the area, then essentially the suffering of those in the neighbourhood of the factory would be ignored. This is called the **TYRANNY OF THE MAJORITY**.

CAN HUMAN BEINGS FLOURISH IN THE CONTEXT OF CAPITALISM AND CONSUMERISM?

Capitalism relies on a **COMPETITIVE INDIVIDUALISM** which can foster great social inequalities. In the context of rampant consumerism, demand for cheap products will mean poor working conditions for many.

Equally, the **CONSUMERISM** of modern developed societies can foster a selfishness and ennui, a kind of spiritual void, which people attempt to fill with more material goods. In such a context it becomes difficult to experience the world as gift, to be thankful with little, and to understand one's self as a being created for a deeper purpose than material acquisition.

As previously mentioned, wealth can be viewed in ways other than the purely monetary kind. The right kind of wealth-creation might actually enable human flourishing. What might that look like?

A system devised in the early twentieth century by **G K CHESTERTON**, **HILAIRE BELLOC** and others called **DISTRIBUTISM**, aimed at promoting an economic vision in which human flourishing is central. Some of its key ideas are:

- **LEVEL THE FIELD** - As long as capital is in the hands of a few massive corporations, inequalities and injustices will continue; far more people could be given incentives to go into business, and this would create more equitable conditions.

- **THE INVISIBLE HAND OF THE MARKET** - Should not be allowed to run things; state control would have to be stronger and more prevalent to stop irresponsible speculation, and make sure businesses were run ethically.

- **THE CATHOLIC CHURCH** - Has promoted in many of its encyclicals a vision very similar to this; for instance, in Rerum Novarum, Pope Leo XIII laid out fundamental principles for the relationship between labour and capital, including: the dignity of the human person, the common good, subsidiarity, participation, solidarity, the right of private property and the universal destination of goods. These principles form the backbone of **CATHOLIC SOCIAL TEACHING**.

NEED MORE HELP ON BUSINESS ETHICS?

Use your phone to scan this QR code

Lightning Source UK Ltd.
Milton Keynes UK
UKOW05f0939160317

296752UK00002B/72/P